NASCAR

PORTLAND
INTERNATIONAL
RACEWAY

To Jeromy,

This story belongs
to all of us!

PORTLAND
INTERNATIONAL
RACEWAY

Jeff Zurschmeide

ARCADIA
PUBLISHING

Published by Arcadia Publishing
Charleston, South Carolina

Printed in the United States of America

Library of Congress Control Number: 2013936576

For all general information, please contact Arcadia Publishing:
Telephone 843-853-2070
Fax 843-853-0044
E-mail sales@arcadiapublishing.com
For customer service and orders:
Toll-Free 1-888-313-2665

Visit us on the Internet at www.arcadiapublishing.com

NASCAR® and NASCAR Library Collection are registered trademarks of the National
Association for Stock Car Auto Racing, Inc.

*In honor of Bob Dunsmore—the man who
saw it all and recorded it for history.*

CONTENTS

ACKNOWLEDGMENTS

This book would not have been possible without the cooperation of the Portland, Oregon, racing community. Specifically, Mike Bell and the Oregon Motorsports Museum Association (OMMA) have collected and store a great deal of information on car and motorcycle racing at Portland International Raceway (PIR). Greg Rollin of Supercars Unlimited performed all the research on PIR drag racing history. Ron Wylder provided all the information on the history of PIR motocross. Any errors and omissions are strictly my fault.

Dale LaFollette and Mark Wigginton have been the managers of PIR since 1973 and have kept a written and photographic record of events while building the park into a world-class facility. Dane Pitarresi and Todd Harris of the ProDrive Racing School have been teaching people to drive and race safely at PIR for decades. Bob Ames has been indispensable to the track in moments of crisis and opportunity.

None of the history of PIR could have happened without the members of Cascade Sports Car Club, Oregon Region Sports Car Club of America (SCCA), Oregon Motorcycle Road Racing Association, National Hot Rod Association (NHRA) drag racers, Portland Karting Association, Oregon Bicycle Racing Association, Team Continental, Alfa Romeo Owners of Oregon, Oregon Region Porsche Club of America, the Portland Rose Festival Foundation, and many other users who keep the heartbeat of activity going at PIR.

This book includes photographs from Doug Berger, Jerry Boone, John Bradshaw, Carol Brown, Dave Brunn, Joe Cantrell, the estate of Bob Dunsmore, Ken Dwinnell, Chris Greenwood, Bob Mead, George Olson, Bob Pengraph, Dick Powers, Stacy Sinclair, and many anonymous photographers whose work is now curated by OMMA and PIR. All photographers retain copyright to their work.

INTRODUCTION

About 15,000 years ago at the end of the last ice age, an ice dam melted in what is now Montana, releasing an expansive lake into a flash flood. The raging waters swept westward to the Pacific Ocean, carving out the Columbia River Gorge and carrying an immense quantity of silt and gravel in their wake. At the confluence of the Willamette and Columbia Rivers, much of that earth came to rest in a low-lying swampy delta.

When William Overton and Asa Lovejoy founded Portland in 1843, the partners staked their new claim south of the delta on the solid western bank of the Willamette. Twenty years earlier, the Hudson's Bay Company had founded Vancouver on the north shore of the Columbia. The delta that lay in between was thought to be useless.

When the United States entered the World War II, Portland and Vancouver were already centers for shipbuilding, and a new community was quickly established near the shipyards. Vanport went from empty fields to the largest public housing project in America in just six months, as workers were brought in from all over the United States to aid in the war effort.

After the war, Vanport languished until 1948, when a massive flood breached the dikes and literally washed away the town. When the floodwaters receded, all that remained was a network of streets. The federal government deeded the land to the City of Portland for use as a public park.

Throughout the 1950s, the empty Vanport streets were a popular site for clandestine racing. But in 1961, visionaries in the Portland Jaycees, Cascade Sports Car Club, and the Portland Rose Festival banded together to create the Rose Cup Races—a legitimate competition event backed by the city.

Auto racing in Portland stretched back as far as 1905, when local magnate E. Henry Wemme organized hill climb races in Portland's west hills. Portland was the site of the first-ever US national championship road race in 1909, aptly named the Wemme Trophy. The 1909 event was organized by the Portland Rose Festival and sanctioned by the fledgling AAA. Throughout the first half of the century, race tracks came and went, at Jantzen Beach, the Rose City Golf Course, and across North Denver Avenue at Portland Speedway. But West Delta Park was a new creation, a proper road-racing course within the city limits of Portland.

The swampy land and sloughs of West Delta Park became the home of Portland International Raceway (PIR). This unique track remains a city-owned park built on the ruins of the wartime community of Vanport, Oregon. (Courtesy of Dick Powers.)

Harry Cohen crashed his car, but was not injured, during the 1909 Wemme Trophy race. The 15-mile circuit started on Stark Street headed west, then turned south on SE Ninety-sixth Avenue in Portland, then east on Division Street, and then north on 223rd Avenue in Gresham back to Stark. (Courtesy of Dale LaFollette.)

The town of Vanport was not engineered for the long run, and in 1948, the levees burst and almost the entire town was washed away. When the waters receded and the wreckage was cleared, only the bones of the town remained. The people of Vanport mostly resettled farther to the south in Portland. (Courtesy of PIR.)

This picture shows the area that is now the south paddock at PIR. The foundations of the water tower (at left) were later buried under the low hill that overlooks turn No. 11. (Courtesy of PIR.)

The floodwaters lifted the temporary worker housing buildings off their foundations and smashed the structures together. The city of Vanport was a total loss except for its roads. (Courtesy of PIR.)

One

Days of Wine and Roses

In the spring of 1961, Cascade Sports Car Club race chairman Max Schultz had an idea to approach the Portland Rose Festival Association about a sports car race on the old Vanport streets. Dick Miller of Cascade Sports Car Club approached the Portland Jaycees and the City of Portland and got approval to hold a sports car race on Saturday, June 11. Some visionary at the Rose Festival wrote "First Annual Rose Cup Races" on the event program.

Dale LaFollette has been involved with PIR since the beginning. As a young man, he was a member of the Portland Jaycees and volunteered at the first Rose Cup. LaFollette later went on to become the manager of Portland International Raceway from 1973 to 1995.

"The idea was to get the racing off the streets. Someone in the Jaycees noticed that the Vanport roads all connect and nobody could think of a reason to say no," LaFollette says.

The roads that made up the race course were crumbling, and drivers were in danger of dropping their cars in the swampy sloughs that surrounded the Vanport streets. Divers with scuba gear were stationed near the water to retrieve drivers from their cars in the event of a water landing—and they did have to pull a few out of the sloughs. "It was a bunch of crowned roads and it was awful. There was a wooden bridge covered with asphalt over the slough," LaFollette says.

The Rose Cup Races established the viability of a permanent sports car racing course in North Portland, and soon drag racing, motorcycle racing, and other events came to be held at the facility. At times, the course was known as Auto Sports Park but more often simply West Delta Park. In 1966, a consortium of clubs known as the Oregon Racing Federation developed a master plan to construct a drag strip, powerboat racing lagoon, a dirt oval track, and an expanded sports car racing circuit—the new facility was to be called Portland International Raceways.

Under the direction of track manager Al Beachell of the Multnomah Hot Rod Council, an eighth-mile drag strip was completed in 1968, which was extended to a quarter-mile strip in 1971. The sports car racing circuit also received new pavement and improvements in this era, but the remaining elements of the project were abandoned.

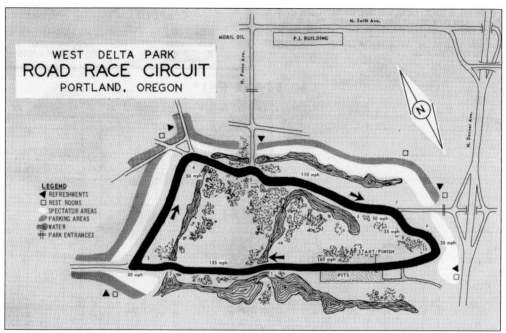

This is the track map from the original 1961 Rose Cup program. The left-side straight is now part of the Heron Lakes golf course. The front and straights are approximately where they remain today. (Courtesy of Portland Rose Festival Foundation.)

Shirley Sleeper's TR3 ended up in the slough at the first Rose Cup Races. Sleeper was not injured. Divers Al Beale and Gerald Mulvaney assisted in pulling the car out of the water. Note the poor condition of the asphalt at the trackside. (Courtesy of PIR.)

Here is the frontstretch at PIR, looking east. (Courtesy of OMMA.)

Looking east is the frontstretch at the 1962 Rose Cup. For this second annual event, the track was called "Auto Sports Park." (Courtesy of PIR.)

Jerry Grant (No. 78) won both the 1961 and 1962 Rose Cup Races in this three-liter Ferrari, owned by Dick Hahn of Yakima, Washington. (Courtesy of OMMA.)

Turn No. 5 on the original course was located where drivers find turn No. 8 on the current course. (Courtesy of OMMA.)

Bill Krause in the white Maserati leads Jerry Grant in the red Ferrari in the 1962 Rose Cup Races. (Courtesy of PIR.)

An unidentified driver inspects his Lotus in turn No. 4. (Courtesy of OMMA.)

Don Rudberg in the No. 255 Sprite leads Bill Rudberg in the No. 254 MG Midget and Roger Stillick in the No. 363 Triumph Spitfire in the 1967 Rose Cup Races. (Courtesy of PIR.)

Pictured is the front row of a Cascade Sports Car Club I Production race in the mid-1960s. The driver of No. 119 is Bob Hansen. (Courtesy of OMMA.)

After the first few years, Cascade Sports Car Club moved the start-finish line to the frontstretch. The track was still limited to the narrow and crumbling Vanport streets. (Courtesy of OMMA.)

Bill Krause (No. 53) of Compton, California, was one of the leading contenders in the early days of the Rose Cup in his Birdcage Maserati. Krause was famous for winning the Riverside Times GP in this car in 1960. (Courtesy of OMMA.)

Here is another view of the frontstretch in the early days. The current south paddock is located on the right, and the infield paddock is on the left. (Courtesy of PIR.)

Gerry Bruihl (No. 41) of Portland prepares for a victory lap in his Fiat-powered Lotus 23. (Courtesy of Doug Berger.)

Rose Festival queen Sally Swift takes a parade lap before the 1965 Rose Cup. (Courtesy of Doug Berger.)

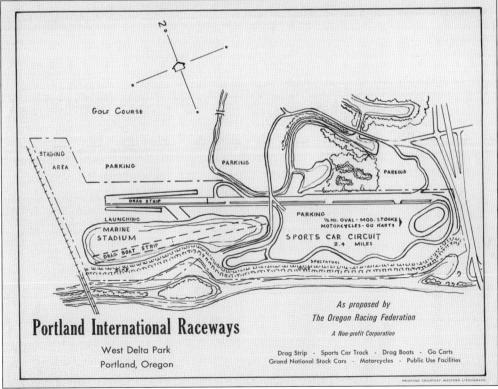

This ambitious plan for a new facility, called Portland International Raceways, was proposed to the Portland City Council in 1966. The plan was developed by a consortium of track users and included a completely redesigned road course, drag boat lagoon, dirt oval track, and dedicated drag strip. The plan was never adopted. (Courtesy of PIR.)

Here, Maeda Rohr (No. 78) drives her Porsche 356 in the 1966 G Production race. (Courtesy of the Dunsmore Archive.)

Formula cars are traversing the back side of PIR, near what is now turn No. 8. (Courtesy of the Dunsmore Archive.)

Here, a big Austin-Healey, driven by Ray Gentile Jr. (No. 433), recovers from a spin while the MGA of Bill Hill (No. 113) drives by. Gentile was not injured and completed the race. (Courtesy of the Dunsmore Archive.)

Mac Russell (No. 104) of Seattle celebrates a victory lap for his Triumph TR-3. Russell had just won the 1966 Rose Cup F Improved Production class. (Courtesy of the Dunsmore Archive.)

Here, Bob Hasson won the D Production race in his No. 7 Sunbeam Tiger (center), gridded between Ray Gentile Jr. (left) and an unidentified Austin-Healey 3000. (Courtesy of the Dunsmore Archive.)

Cascade Sports Car Club officials, including starter Cal Watson in his trademark checkered shirt, enjoy the day at the 1966 Rose Cup Races. (Courtesy of the Dunsmore Archive.)

Pictured are Gary Wright in the No. 356 Porsche Carrera and an unidentified driver in the No. 16 Lotus 7. (Courtesy of the Dunsmore Archive.)

Formula Vees are seen rounding turn No. 5 at the 1966 Rose Cup Races. (Courtesy of Doug Berger.)

Present-day turn No. 10, which comes off the backstretch into the east-end area, was known as "the Circus." (Courtesy of PIR.)

The driver of No. 119 is Bob Hansen. Fred Kawabata is also on the front row in the No. 152 Sprite. The nose of the No. 11 MGA of Bruce Baggett is visible in the second row, along with the No. 275 Sprite of John Swanson. (Courtesy of PIR.)

Fred Harris leads in the No. 285 Corvette Sting Ray, followed by the No. 198 Jag XKE of Stanley Glaros and the No. 0 Corvette of Nick Cox. (Courtesy of PIR.)

Bob Daly in the No. 3 Porsche 356 leads Bill Stevens in the No. 100 Austin-Healey and Jim Lamb in the No. 57 MGB. (Courtesy of PIR.)

Dewey Harless crosses the track at the start-finish line of PIR around 1966. The people gathered on the riser are the timing and scoring team, tracking cars by stopwatch. (Courtesy of PIR.)

Monte Shelton's No. 57 Lola race car is pictured with the 1967 Rose Festival court at the Oregon Zoo. (Courtesy of Doug Berger.)

Here, Gerry Bruihl (No. 41) drives his Enduro-Special with a two-liter Coventry Climax engine in the 1967 Rose Cup. (Courtesy of Doug Berger.)

In this view looking west at the start-finish tower around 1967–1969, longtime racing steward John Bradshaw (far right) is walking toward the camera. (Courtesy of OMMA.)

Bob Hasson in his No. 7 Sunbeam Tiger (left) races with Todd Webb in his Lotus Elan at the 1966 Rose Cup. (Courtesy of OMMA.)

"Angry John" Antons (No. 89) raced this Shelby Cobra unopposed in the A Production class in 1966. (Courtesy of OMMA.)

Ray Gentile Jr. in the Austin-Healey (No. 433) leads a Lotus 7 and a Formula Vee. (Courtesy of the Dunsmore Archive.)

Mike Eyerly is on pole in his No. 14 Porsche 356 with Gary Wright in the No. 8 Porsche next to him in the small bore production group at the 1968 Rose Cup Races. (Courtesy of Doug Berger.)

Here is a line of sports cars at the 1969 Rose Cup Races. The No. 4 Porsche 906 of Mike Fisher is on the right. Monte Shelton's No. 57 Lola T-70 is in the middle of the line. (Courtesy of Doug Berger.)

Starter Cal Watson (checkered shirt) and his crew work a Cascade Sports Car Club race in the late 1960s. (Courtesy of Doug Berger.)

Here, fans gather on the east bank to watch the races. Noted formula car driver Win Casey is shown at center. Roger Huntley is shown wearing his hat. (Courtesy of Doug Berger.)

Here is the Cascade Sports Car Club timing and scoring crew. Volunteers used stopwatches to time laps and wrote down the order in which cars crossed the timing line. (Courtesy of Doug Berger.)

Race control was managed from this camper, with headsets connected to a closed-circuit communications loop around the track. Oregon Region Sports Car Club of America (SCCA) regional executive Dan Allen is seated on the right. (Courtesy of Doug Berger.)

Race officials are seen taking a break in the heat of the afternoon. (Courtesy of Doug Berger.)

Racing prepares to get underway at the 1969 Rose Cup Races. (Courtesy of the Dunsmore Archive.)

Bill Craine (No. 89) sits in his Datsun roadster at the 1969 Rose Cup. Craine went on to race Corvettes in Trans-Am. (Courtesy of the Dunsmore Archive.)

Ted Mathey (No. 135) drives his 427 Corvette at the 1969 Rose Cup Races. (Courtesy of OMMA.)

Two

PIR Growing Up

In the early 1970s, Portland International Raceway was a solid fixture in West Delta Park. The drag strip along the frontstretch had been improved, and better pavement was laid down for the sports car circuit, along with the first freeway-style guardrails around the track.

Improvements began in the late 1960s with an eye toward big-time drag racing. In 1969, the track was shortened due to bad pavement in the west end, and the drag strip was repaved. By 1971, the track had taken on its current, familiar shape after a thorough repaving and realignment. The City of Portland, the Portland Rose Festival Association, and the Oregon Racing Federation funded the improvements. The new pavement was inaugurated at the 1971 Rose Festival Drag Races, followed a week later by the Rose Cup Races, now sanctioned by Oregon Region Sports Car Club of America.

In the early 1970s, the Rose Cup was a free format race for any cars with enclosed fenders. The entries included all the fastest production cars of the day, and the top V8-powered sports cars from the Can-Am Series.

In 1973, track manager Al Beachell retired. Mike Campbell served briefly, and then Dale LaFollette was hired to direct the facility. LaFollette managed PIR through its most exciting growth years as International Motor Sports Association (IMSA), Champ Car, and the Rose Festival improved the PIR facility to handle the huge crowds drawn by professional racing in that era.

In 1974, the PIR tower was built in the south paddock area near the combination pit road and drag race launch pad. The existing timing tower was moved into the infield for use with the motocross course.

In 1977, the south paddock was paved with funds from the Portland Rose Festival Association and user clubs including Team Continental, Oregon Region SCCA, and Cascade Sports Car Club.

The first SCCA Trans-Am 2.5 Challenge Series race took place in 1972, but in 1975, the Rose Cup became a Trans-Am Series event, and Trans-Am remained the Rose Cup feature until the arrival of Champ Car in 1984. With Champ Car as the premier professional event, the Rose Cup returned to amateur status as an SCCA event.

In 1978, the IMSA Camel GT Series arrived, and PIR started another era of growth.

"IMSA in its heyday was unbelievable racing. You had half a dozen factories involved and they were all going," LaFollete says.

Dick Losk leads the A Sports Racer field in his No. 20 McLaren. The No. 92 McLaren of Ted Peterson is also visible among several unidentified cars. (Courtesy of PIR.)

The No. 87 McLaren of Gregg Peterson leads a pack of A Sedan muscle cars through what is now turn No. 12. (Courtesy of PIR.)

This Sceptre-Fiat D Sports Racer was campaigned by Bill Stephens (No. 18). (Courtesy of PIR.)

This No. 69 Lola sports car belonged to Eric Anderson. Before 1977, the south paddock at PIR was still grass and gravel, and drivers had to work on their cars as best they could. (Courtesy of PIR.)

Ted Mathey in his No. 35 Corvette leads Joe Chamberlain in the No. 76 Camaro and Bill Pendleton in a No. 56 Mercury Cougar through what is now turn No. 12. (Courtesy of PIR.)

A big group of Formula Fords entertains the crowd at a Rose Cup Races in the early 1970s. (Courtesy of PIR.)

Rich Sloma (No. 22) takes a wide line through turn No. 12 as Ted Mathey (No. 35) approaches. (Courtesy of PIR.)

The No. 92 McLaren, a sports car of Ted Peterson, is seen at the 1970 Rose Cup Races. (Courtesy of PIR.)

An unidentified driver (No. 22) takes a Formula C victory lap at the 1971 Rose Cup Races. (Courtesy of PIR.)

Here is Monte Shelton's No. 57 Chevron formula car. Monte is walking up from the right, and 2008 Rose Cup winner Neil Shelton is steering his dad's car. (Courtesy of PIR.)

John L. Matteson (No. 75) drove this D Sedan Mini in the early 1970s. (Courtesy of PIR.)

Monte Shelton is ready to race in his No. 57 Chevron. Monte won his first Rose Cup in 1972 and then won six more times to become the winningest driver in Rose Cup history. (Photograph by Bob Mead.)

Don Korner (No. 28) is seen in his F Production Austin-Healey Sprite. (Courtesy of PIR.)

Hal Roren (No. 39) is pictured in his F Production Alfa Romeo Spider. (Courtesy of PIR.)

J.D. Rogers (No. 2) is shown in his F Production Datsun 2000 roadster. (Courtesy of PIR.)

Here is Alex Ceres (No. 50) in his G Production Alfa Romeo Giulietta Sprint. (Courtesy of PIR.)

Formula Vees are coming down the backstretch. (Courtesy of Doug Berger.)

Formula Vees are rounding what is now turn No. 12, with the newly built Blitz Tower in the background. The tower was built over the winter in 1974. The building that houses the bathrooms and the Fast Track Café is also visible in the background. (Courtesy of Doug Berger.)

Monte Shelton (No. 57) is on his way to winning the 1974 Rose Cup Races in his Lola M8F. 1974 was the last year for the free formula Rose Cup. In 1975, Trans-Am became the Rose Cup group. (Courtesy of the Dunsmore Archive.)

Arnstein Loyning in the No. 22 and Pete Darr in his No. 24 Titan Mk6 Formula Fords made a great-looking team. (Courtesy of the Dunsmore Archive.)

PIR booster and Rose Festival auto racing chairman Bob Ames (left) converses with Carroll Shelby (center) and Al Stephens, founder of the Forest Grove Concours. (Courtesy of PIR.)

Doug Barbour in the No. 97 Datsun leads Tom Nelson in the right-hand drive Sprite and the rest of the small bore production group at the 1974 Rose Cup Races. (Courtesy of PIR.)

Paul Newman came to PIR with the Trans-Am Series as a driver and then returned with Champ Car as a team owner. (Courtesy of Doug Berger.)

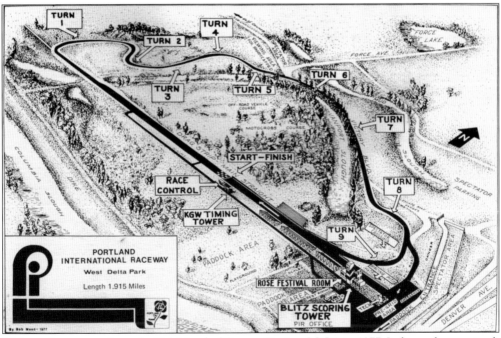

This track map was drawn by Bob Mead of Oregon Region SCCA in 1977. It shows the new track configuration created in 1971. Note that the Festival Curves chicane had not yet been added to the frontstretch. (Courtesy of PIR.)

PIR, as well as sports car racing in general, depends on the skill and professionalism of its crew of flagging and communications volunteers. (Courtesy of the Dunsmore Archive.)

Win Casey (No. 98) in his Audi Fox leads the small bore production and sedan group in the 1983 Rose Cup Races. (Courtesy of the Dunsmore Archive.)

Paul Newman races his No. 33 Datsun 280ZX in the 1983 Trans-Am Rose Cup Races. (Courtesy of the Dunsmore Archive.)

As the field comes through turn No. 5, Greg Sherick has the pole position in the No. 11 Triumph Spitfire with the rest of the small bore GT and production field gathered up behind him. (Courtesy of the Dunsmore Archive.)

Paul Newman (No. 33) leads the field, including the No. 8 Mercury Capri of Tom Gloy, in the 1983 Rose Cup Trans-Am race. (Courtesy of the Dunsmore Archive.)

Willy T. Ribbs is on his way to winning the 1983 Rose Cup Trans-Am race in the No. 28 Camaro. Paul Miller is behind Ribbs in the No. 36 Porsche. (Courtesy of the Dunsmore Archive.)

PIR flagging and communications workers occasionally honor winning drivers with a "Dover Wave," in which all flags are waved during a victory lap. Getting a Dover Wave is a very big deal for any race car driver at Portland. (Courtesy of the Dunsmore Archive.)

Willy T. Ribbs celebrates his victory at the 1983 Rose Cup Trans-Am event. Bill Hildick of the Portland Rose Festival is driving. Shortly after this photograph was taken, Ribbs poured the beer on Hildick's head. (Courtesy of the Dunsmore Archive.)

Three

FULL FLOWER

1984 was a watershed year in the history of PIR because of the arrival of Championship Auto Racing Teams (CART, or just Champ Car). Champ Car's stringent race-course certification brought a host of changes to the facility, starting with the now-famous Festival Curves. These three new turns were added to the frontstretch to slow down the Champ Cars and have since become a feature turn combination for PIR. The first curves were gentle and later deepened to further reduce speeds.

CART required a faster pit with closer paddock space than the south paddock could accommodate, so an area of the infield was paved and made into the "pro pits." Additional concrete walls were added with tall catch fences.

For 1985, the walk-over bridge was added to provide access to the Champ Car pit and paddock area. Additional grandstands were added over the years to accommodate the spectators at the Champ Car events.

In the mid-1990s, a new scoring and control tower was built in the infield. Made from shipping containers and featuring external staircases, the new tower features storage on the ground level and control rooms on the second and third floors.

After Champ Car arrived, the Trans-Am race moved to Champ Car weekend as a support race. Since that time, the Rose Cup Races have remained with the Sports Car Club of America as a race for local and regional amateur drivers.

Manager Dale LaFollette retired in 1995 and was replaced by Mark Wigginton, who has managed track operations since that time.

During this era, PIR has become host to a variety of different events. Since the early 1970s, a motocross course in the infield has seen weekly use. But events as diverse as autocross, bicycling, swap meets, cruise-ins, running races, and even a Christmas lights show all share the park, delivering 365 "use days" per year.

PIR was briefly threatened in the early 2000s, first by a proposed music amphitheater to be built in the infield and then by political challenges with an unsympathetic city council. Just as during the fuel crisis of 1973, in the mid-2000s Portland's Mayor Tom Potter focused on the race track. He proposed a study to see if the current track could be shut down and the entire facility moved west to the shipping terminal district—a plan that would be far too expensive to complete. The move led to the creation of Friends of PIR, an advocacy and service group with thousands of members in Portland and the surrounding areas.

PIR is pictured in the mid-1980s. The first chicane on the frontstretch has been created but it is a gentle curve that does not slow down the cars very much. The infield paddock has been paved, and the crossover bridge is present. (Courtesy of PIR.)

Monte Shelton (No. 57) dominated the 1980s in the car that came to be known as Old Blue. Shelton won the Rose Cup in 1984, 1986, and 1988. (Courtesy of PIR.)

Flagging and communication workers wave race car drivers onto the track at the 1985 Rose Cup Races. The new crossover bridge is visible in the background. (Courtesy of PIR.)

After the arrival of Champ Car, the Rose Cup returned to its local club racing roots with the standard format of GT1-GT2-GT3 and Super Production classes. (Courtesy of PIR.)

Dan Hall (No. 77) was a founding member of Oregon Region SCCA and a mainstay of PIR's club racing program. (Courtesy of PIR.)

Monte Shelton collected his fifth Rose Cup win in 1986, driving his trademark Super Production class Porsche. (Courtesy of PIR.)

In the modern era, the Rose Cup Races feature fast V8-powered tube-framed cars running in SCCA's most powerful classes. (Courtesy of PIR.)

The crew members at PIR's turn No. 12 have to stay on their toes, as cars often slide into the tire wall right in front of the turn station. (Courtesy of PIR.)

Trans-Am remained a draw almost to the end of the Champ Car series in Portland. In this photograph, Tommy Kendall car waits on pit road for the 1990 event. (Courtesy of George Olson.)

In this east-facing aerial shot from 1992, one can see that the chicane has been deepened and sharpened to further slow cars. In this era, the center of the chicane was filled with a pea gravel bed. That pea gravel tended to trap cars that failed to make the first corner. (Courtesy of PIR.)

In 1993, stunt pilot Ray Richter made history by flying a light plane underneath the PIR track-crossing bridge. The event was recorded on film and has never been repeated. (Courtesy of Doug Berger.)

A rare angle and a clear day show Mount St. Helens overlooking the track. When the volcano erupted in 1980, the track was covered in ash, forcing drivers and workers to don respirators; it also forced the cancellation of events for several months. Gordon Barron's 914-6 (No. 76) is shown in the foreground. (Courtesy of Doug Berger.)

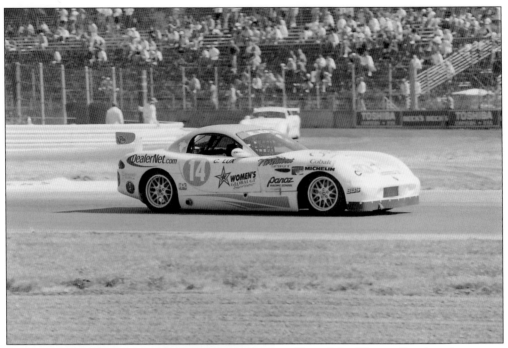

Part of the Champ Car show in 1999 was the Women's Global GT Series, raced in identical Panoz sports cars. Portland driver Cindi Lux (No. 14) won the series championship. (Courtesy of Doug Berger.)

Cindi Lux is the daughter of Dick Hahn, owner of the car that won the first two Rose Cup Races. Lux also holds the title for the highest-finishing woman in Rose Cup history, with her third-place finish in 2011. (Photograph by Jeff Zurschmeide.)

Trans-Am continued to race in Portland until the series went on hiatus after the 2005 season. The event returned to Portland when the series was revived in 2009. (Courtesy of George Olson.)

Starting with a win in 1995, Steve Hodge (No. 88) became the second-winningest driver in Rose Cup history, collecting a total of six victories by 2006. (Photograph by Jeff Zurschmeide.)

Flagging and communications officials Erin Ebelmesser and Lee Casebeer work the corners at an Oregon Region SCCA event. (Courtesy of the Dunsmore Archive.)

The 2005 Rose Cup was controversial because of Monte Shelton's entry in the No. 57 Porsche 962. However, the car was ruled a legal production car per FIA classifications, and Shelton's seventh Rose Cup victory stood. (Courtesy of the Dunsmore Archive.)

In 2007, Todd Harris (No. 24) won the Rose Cup for the first time. Harris operates ProDrive Racing School at PIR and is known as one of the track's most skilled drivers. (Photograph by Jeff Zurschmeide.)

After Champ Car ceased operations in 2007, Mazda promoted two annual Mazda Grand Prix of Portland events, featuring classes such as Star Mazda formula cars and the VW TDI Cup, shown here. Although the events featured great racing, they were discontinued after two years. (Photograph by Jeff Zurschmeide.)

PIR underwent a much-needed repaving in the fall of 2007, making substantial changes to turns Nos. 5, 6, 7, and 10. In some places, the pavement replaced had been in use since the last full repaving in 1970. (Photograph by Jeff Zurschmeide.)

In 2008, Neil Shelton won the Rose Cup driving the family Porsche 962, making him the only second-generation winner of the trophy. The trophy was presented by his father, Monte Shelton. (Photograph by Jeff Zurschmeide.)

2009 brought a one-time return of the SCCA Pro Racing Trans-Am Series as the Rose Cup event. Tomy Drissi (leading in No. 5) won the race that year. (Photograph by Jeff Zurschmeide.)

2010 marked the 50th annual running of the Rose Cup Races, and many past winners were on hand for the event, including, from left to right, three-time winner Brian Richards, 2007 winner Todd Harris, 1961–1962 winner Jerry Grant, three-time winner Matt Crandall, and seven-time winner Monte Shelton. (Photograph by Jeff Zurschmeide.)

Monte Shelton (right) and Jerry Grant share memories at the 2010 Rose Cup. Shelton entered the 1961 event in an MGA Roadster. (Photograph by Jeff Zurschmeide.)

In the modern era, the Oregon Bicycle Racing Association uses PIR on Monday and Tuesday evenings, riding on the racing surface. Bicyclists are an important voice with the City of Portland on behalf of all track users. (Courtesy of Friends of PIR.)

Go-Karts and the Portland Karting Association are other key track users, running several major events each year. (Courtesy of Chris Greenwood.)

In the mid-2000s, the Beaches Cruise-in moved to PIR, which often draws up to 800 hot rods, customs, and classics each Wednesday evening throughout the summer. (Photograph by Jeff Zurschmeide.)

Another activity at the track is semiannual automotive swap meets. These open-air automotive markets are held in the spring and fall and constitute major revenue streams for the facility. (Photograph by Jeff Zurschmeide.)

Cascade Sports Car Club operates a signature eight-hour Enduro race each fall. This race features the only true Le Mans start on the West Coast. Drivers line up on the pit wall and run to their cars when the signal is given. (Photograph by Jeff Zurschmeide.)

The Oregon Trail Rally races on some of the original pavement left over from Vanport around the perimeter of the current track facility. Some of this decaying asphalt was used in the first Rose Cup Races. In this photograph, driver Mark Tabor and codriver Kevin Poirier slide onto the old frontstretch. (Photograph by Jeff Zurschmeide.)

The Oregon Trail Rally is the only event of its kind to run stages inside the city limits of a major American metropolis. About 5,000 fans turn out each May to watch rally teams such as driver Paul Eklund and codriver Jeff Price (shown here, No. 233) drive at PIR. (Photograph by Jeff Zurschmeide.)

Club racing by Oregon Region Sports Car Club of America provides a steady pulse of activity at PIR. In this photograph, Dave Rice (No. 37) leads Tom Burt (No. 45) in SCCA's popular Spec Racer Ford class. (Photograph by Jeff Zurschmeide.)

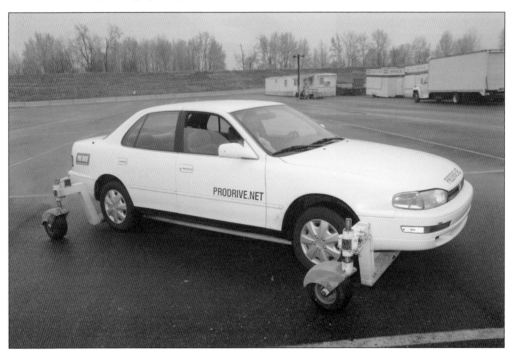

In addition to teaching racing and high-performance driving, ProDrive teaches safe driving in rainy, snowy, and icy conditions year-round at PIR. This is accomplished with the use of a specially equipped SkidCar. (Photograph by Jeff Zurschmeide.)

From October 31 to November 1, 2009, PIR hosted the Chump Car World Series for the first and only 24-hour race in track history. Limited to low-cost cars with limited preparation, the series encourages high-fun and low-stress racing. (Courtesy of Stacy Sinclair.)

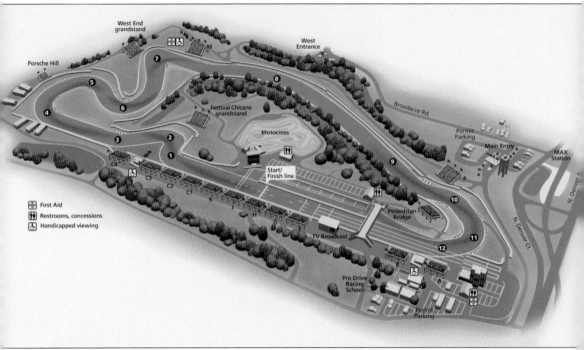

PIR is shown as it is configured today. Compare the path through turns Nos. 5–7 with previous maps for a sense of how the track was changed in the 2007 repaving. (Courtesy of PIR.)

Four

NASCAR AT PIR

With Portland Speedway located just across the freeway, NASCAR racing waited until 1986 to come to Portland International Raceway. But when the stock cars arrived, fan response was tremendous. A road course offers entirely different challenges to drivers compared to an oval, and PIR is no exception.

The NASCAR series that have raced at PIR have gone by many names between 1986 and 2012. In all, PIR has seen seven NASCAR Northwest Series races, two NASCAR Craftsman (now Camping World) Truck Series races, and five races in the NASCAR K&N Pro Series West.

Northwest stock car racing legend Herschel McGriff won the first-ever race in what is now the NASCAR K&N Pro Series West at PIR, in a race that also included notable Trans-Am driver George Follmer. Nine years later, Mark Martin won the first NASCAR Northwest Series event. Dale Jarrett was also part of that race. The NASCAR Northwest Series came to Portland once a year from 1995 to 1998, raced twice at PIR in 2000, and then returned in 2001 for one final race.

Greg Biffle participated in several NASCAR Northwest Series events before winning the first NASCAR Craftsman (now Camping World) Truck Series event at PIR in 1999. That event was also notable for the number of Trans-Am and IMSA Series drivers who appeared, including Boris Said and Ron Fellows. Another native Portland NASCAR driver, Mike Bliss, also competed in that race. PIR's racing school owner Dane Pitarresi competed in both years of the NASCAR Craftsman (now Camping World) Truck Series at PIR.

NASCAR returned to PIR in 2009 with the NASCAR K&N Pro Series West. The event was created by local businessman and racing promoter Chris Evans as a way to bring NASCAR back to Portland. Evans's own Great American Stockcar Series (GASS) was the key support race at these weekends. Evans billed the annual event the "Salute to the Troops 125" and always featured a large military and patriotic presence. Four races have been held at PIR under this title.

In addition to appearing at NASCAR-sanctioned events, retired NASCAR race cars are an important part of the Portland Historic Races each summer. For these events, retired NASCAR machines are lovingly restored to the livery they bore for a particular race—typically the best finish for the car—and the new owner/drivers put on demonstration races for the fans.

Jim Bown (No. 02) leads Terry Fisher (No. 57) in the 1986 Motorcraft 300 race in what is now known as the NASCAR K&N Pro Series West. (Courtesy of the PIR archive.)

NASCAR drivers often found the gravel in the Festival Curves chicane. Turn No. 1 is a challenge for brakes and tires. (Courtesy of Doug Berger.)

Mark Martin is seen at the 1995 Trendwest Resorts 100 NASCAR Northwest Series race. This event was Martin's first victory in the series. (Courtesy of Doug Berger.)

Martin (No. 6) won the 1995 NASCAR Northwest Series event driving this Ford for Roush. His margin of victory over Ken Pederson was .0002 seconds. (Courtesy of Doug Berger.)

Mark Martin (left) and Dale Jarrett take a moment to relax at the 1995 Trendwest Resorts NASCAR Northwest Series event. (Courtesy of Doug Berger.)

At the 2001 George Morlan 100 NASCAR Northwest Series race, six-time Rose Cup winner Steve Hodge in the No. 88 Chevrolet follows the winning No. 73 Pontiac of Gary Lewis. The No. 42 Chevrolet of Jeff Jefferson is alongside Hodge. (Courtesy of Doug Berger.)

The No. 73 Pontiac of Gary Lewis leads the No. 33 Chevrolet of Kevin Hamlin in the 2001 George Morlan 100 NASCAR Northwest Series race. (Courtesy of Doug Berger.)

The No. 21 Chevrolet of Bill Lawrence leads the No. 39 Chevrolet of Pete Harding at the 2001 George Morlan 100 NASCAR Northwest Series race. (Courtesy of Doug Berger.)

The No. 6 Chevrolet of Wes Rhodes makes a bold pass in turn No. 1 over the No. 28 Chevrolet of Matt Hall at the 2001 George Morlan 100 NASCAR Northwest Series race. (Courtesy of Doug Berger.)

A natural consequence of the gravel pit at turn No. 1 was extensive track sweeping during yellow-flag laps. (Courtesy of Doug Berger.)

Local favorite Steve Hodge (No. 88) won six Rose Cup Races and finished in second place at the 2001 George Morlan 100 NASCAR Northwest Series race. (Courtesy of Doug Berger.)

The No. 18 Chevrolet of John Bender roars up out of the gravel trap at turn No. 1. (Courtesy of Doug Berger.)

The No. 73 Pontiac of Gary Lewis is seen before the start of the 2001 George Morlan 100 NASCAR Northwest Series race. (Courtesy of the Dunsmore Archive.)

Greg Biffle in the No. 50 Ford is on his way to winning the 1999 Grainger Industrial Supply 225K NASCAR Craftsman (now Camping World) Truck Series race. (Courtesy of Doug Berger.)

Greg Biffle (No. 50) celebrates his victory at the 1999 Grainger Industrial Supply 225K NASCAR Craftsman (now Camping World) Truck Series race. As the event sponsor and Biffle's own title sponsor, the victory was especially sweet. (Courtesy of OMMA.)

Trucks are lined up in preparation for the 1999 Grainger Industrial Supply 225K NASCAR Craftsman (now Camping World) Truck Series race. (Courtesy of Chris Greenwood.)

Local favorite and PIR racing school owner Dane Pitarresi drives the No. 78 George Morlan Plumbing truck at the 1999 Grainger Industrial Supply 225K NASCAR Craftsman (now Camping World) Truck Series race. (Courtesy of Chris Greenwood.)

Bryan Reffner plants his No. 3 Johns Manville Chevrolet deep in the pea gravel at the Line-X 225 NASCAR Craftsman (now Camping World) Truck Series race, held April 22, 2000. (Courtesy of Doug Berger.)

Dane Pitarresi locks up a front wheel of the No. 7 SkidCar Systems, Inc. Chevrolet under braking at the 2000 Line-X 225 NASCAR Craftsman (now Camping World) Truck Series race. (Courtesy of Chris Greenwood.)

A crowded field makes its way around turn No. 2 during the 2000 Line-X 225 NASCAR Craftsman (now Camping World) Truck Series race. (Courtesy of Doug Berger.)

Brady Flaherty in the No. 07 Chevrolet sails through turn No. 2 while Kevin Culver (No. 52) recovers from oversteering in the 2011 NASCAR K&N Pro Series West race. (Courtesy of Doug Berger.)

The No. 20 Toyota of Eric Holmes and the No. 6 Ford of Jason Bowles come close to rubbing at turn No. 2 during the Bi-Mart Salute to the Troops 125 NASCAR K&N Pro Series West race in 2009. (Courtesy of Joe Cantrell.)

The No. 6 Ford of Jason Bowles leads a pack through turn No. 12 in the 2009 Bi-Mart Salute to the Troops 125 NASCAR K&N Pro Series West race. (Photograph by Jeff Zurschmeide.)

The No. 14 Ford of Travis Milburn lifts a wheel under hard cornering in turn No. 2 during the 2011 Bi-Mart Salute to the Troops 125 NASCAR K&N Pro Series West race. (Courtesy of Doug Berger.)

The No. 74 Ford of Scott Ivie gets both front wheels off the ground going over the curbing at turn No. 2 of the Festival Curves. (Courtesy of Doug Berger.)

The No. 20 Toyota of Eric Holmes puts on a great show in the Festival Curves at the 2011 Bi-Mart Salute to the Troops 125 NASCAR K&N Pro Series West race. (Courtesy of Doug Berger.)

Greg Rayl lays down the power and lifts a front wheel in his No. 07 Ford at the 2009 Bi-Mart Salute to the Troops 125 NASCAR K&N Pro Series West race. (Courtesy of Joe Cantrell.)

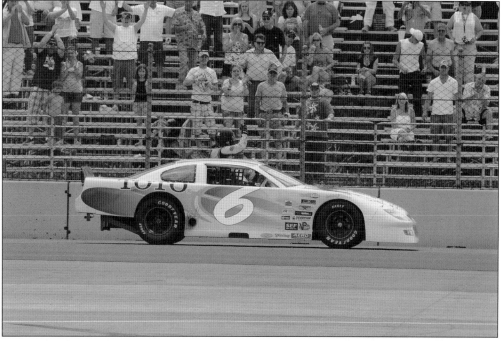

One of Portland's most distinguished race car drivers is Gary Bockman (No. 6), shown here celebrating his win in the 2011 Great American Stockcar Series (GASS) race with the fans at the Bi-Mart Salute to the Troops 125 weekend. (Courtesy of Doug Berger.)

NASCAR K&N Pro Series West cars are lined up before the start of the 2012 Salute to the Troops 125 race. (Photograph by Jeff Zurschmeide.)

Dylan Hutchison gets his No. 5 Chevrolet up on two wheels at the Festival Curves in the 2012 NASCAR K&N Pro Series West Salute to the Troops 125. (Photograph by Jeff Zurschmeide.)

SCCA club racer Eddie Nakato (No. 07) is looking fast in the 2012 NASCAR K&N Pro Series West Salute to the Troops 125 during his rookie season in the series. (Photograph by Jeff Zurschmeide.)

Greg Pursley drove his No. 26 GPM/ Star Nursery/Real Water Ford to victory in the 2012 NASCAR K&N Pro Series West Salute to the Troops 125. (Photograph by Jeff Zurschmeide.)

Retired and restored NASCAR Sprint Cup Series cars of many vintages compete at the annual Portland Historic Races organized by the Historic Motor Sports Association. (Photograph by Jeff Zurschmeide.)

Each of these historic stock cars is restored to its exact livery from a particular race. The new owners take particular pride in keeping these cars in museum-quality condition while racing them around the country. (Photograph by Jeff Zurschmeide.)

Five

CHAMP CAR

No professional racing series has had as much effect on the history of Portland International Raceway as CART, later known as Champ Car. While Trans-Am and IMSA professional racing helped put Portland on the map starting in the 1970s, it was CART's arrival in 1984 that brought PIR to the big time.

CART money paid for substantial improvements around the facility, starting with the frontstretch "pro pits" and the infield paddock. A walk-over bridge across the frontstretch came in 1985. Additional improvements to the curbing, walls, and catch fence brought the track into the modern era of design. New grandstands around the course were constructed to handle the influx of fans. Televising the races brought Portland International Raceway to the attention of viewers around the world.

The list of Portland Champ Car winners reads like a who's who of 24 years of top-drawer formula racing in the United States. Al Unser Jr. won the first Stroh's 200 race on June 17, 1984. Mario Andretti won the next two years, and 1986 marked the first year the race was known as the Budweiser/G.I. Joe's 200. That name stuck through 1999. Along the way, Bobby Rahal, Danny Sullivan, Emerson Fittipaldi, Michael Andretti, Alex Zanardi, Mark Blundell, and Gil de Ferran all put their names on the Portland trophy. Michael Andretti and Al Unser Jr. each won the event three times during that period.

In 2000, the event became known as the Freightliner/G.I. Joe's 200 for two years and then simply the G.I. Joe's 200 until 2006. The final Champ Car event in 2007 was sponsored by Mazda Motor Corporation and named the Mazda Grand Prix of Portland. During the same period, CART went through bankruptcy and emerged as the Champ Car World Series. In the final years of Champ Car racing at PIR, Max Papis, Cristiano da Matta, Adrian Fernandez, AJ Allmendinger, and Sébastien Bourdais all claimed victories.

In addition to track improvements, the CART/Champ Car events helped Portland's auto racing clubs grow and gain critical professional-level experience, leading to the track's reputation for having one of the finest communities of racing officials anywhere in the world. Both Cascade Sports Car Club and Oregon Region SCCA have supported major racing events at PIR for decades and received both financial and experience benefits from their participation.

Here, the SCCA flagging and communications officials push Eddie Cheever's car (No. 15) after the gearbox failed during the 1990 CART 1990 Budweiser/G.I. Joe's 200. (Courtesy of Doug Berger.)

Tom Sneva's car (No. 4) is in the pits at the 1984 Stroh's/G.I. Joe's 200. Sneva finished fifth in the race. (Courtesy of Doug Berger.)

Mario Andretti (No. 3) prepares to drive in the 1984 Stroh's/G.I. Joe's 200. Andretti completed only 13 laps in the race but came back to win in both 1985 and 1986. (Courtesy of Doug Berger.)

Michael (left) and Mario Andretti are pictured before the 1984 race. Michael Andretti finished 12th that year and went on to win in 1990, 1991, and 1992. (Courtesy of Doug Berger.)

Lyn St. James (No. 90) was no stranger to PIR when she raced in the 1993 Budweiser/ G.I. Joe's 200, having raced at the track in both Trans-Am and IMSA events since 1983. (Courtesy of Doug Berger.)

The incomparable Alex Zanardi won the Budweiser/G.I. Joe's 200 in both 1996 and 1998, winning a legion of fans among spectators and fellow race car drivers alike. (Courtesy of the Dunsmore Archive.)

Alex Zanardi performs a spectacular burnout in front of the fans on the PIR frontstretch. After the gravel pit in the Festival Curves was paved, that area became the traditional spot for the victory burnouts. (Courtesy of Doug Berger.)

Mario Andretti returned to PIR many times as a team owner after he ceased active competition. Here, he is shown at the 2001 Freightliner/G.I. Joe's 200. (Courtesy of the Dunsmore Archive.)

Juan Pablo Montoya makes a pit stop during the 2001 Freightliner/G.I. Joe's 200. (Courtesy of the Dunsmore Archive.)

Here, Bryan Herta (No. 77) and Alex Tagliani (No. 33) find the pea gravel during the 2001 Freightliner/G.I. Joe's 200. No one was injured, and both cars continued to race. (Courtesy of the Dunsmore Archive.)

Roberto Moreno leads Dario Franchitti (second) and Tora Takagi (third) through PIR's turn No. 12 during the 2001 Freightliner/G.I. Joe's 200. (Courtesy of the Dunsmore Archive.)

Juan Pablo Montoya is pictured racing during the 1999 Budweiser/G.I. Joe's 200. Montoya finished second in that year's race. (Courtesy of Jerry Boone.)

Rain is often a critical factor at PIR and was an ever-present threat at the Champ Car races, which always took place in mid-June. (Courtesy of the Dunsmore Archive.)

Helio Castroneves (No. 3) takes off from a pit stop in the rain. Note the traditional slick tires have been replaced with deeply grooved tires to provide traction in the water. (Courtesy of the Dunsmore Archive.)

Here, everyone is racing pretty tightly at the start of the 2002 G.I. Joe's 200. Cristiano da Matta would eventually win this race and the 2005 race as well. (Courtesy of the Dunsmore Archive.)

1989 and 1993 PIR winner Emerson Fittipaldi came to the 2003 G.I. Joe's 200 as a team owner of Fittipaldi Dingman Racing. The team fielded Tiago Monteiro, but his day ended early when his car experienced gearbox failure. (Courtesy of the Dunsmore Archive.)

The field takes the green flag for the 2003 G.I. Joe's 200. Paul Tracy is on the left, and Michel Jourdain Jr. is on the right. (Courtesy of Chris Greenwood.)

AJ Allmendinger pulls out after a pit stop during the 2005 G.I. Joe's Grand Prix of Portland. Water was sprayed at the filler port to wash away any spilled methanol fuel. (Courtesy of Bob Pengraph.)

The field heads into turn No. 1 at the start of the 2006 G.I. Joe's Grand Prix of Portland. AJ Allmendinger, who later moved to NASCAR, won the race. (Courtesy of Bob Pengraph.)

The Mazda Atlantic Series followed the Champ Car Series and provided a valuable support race as well as a farm system for Champ Car drivers. This is Dan Selznick (No. 49) at the 2007 Mazda Grand Prix of Portland. (Photograph by Jeff Zurschmeide.)

The Star Mazda Series was another frequent support race for Champ Car. These cars use Mazda rotary engines, where the Atlantics used piston-based Mazda engines. This photograph shows Joel Miller (No. 20) at the 2008 Mazda Grand Prix of Portland. (Photograph by Jeff Zurschmeide.)

Paul Newman also returned to PIR as a team owner, backing Sébastien Bourdais, the winner of the last Champ Car race in Portland. (Courtesy of the Dunsmore Archive.)

Six

IMSA AND ALMS

Trans-Am helped make Portland International Raceway a popular racing destination, but it was IMSA and the Camel GT Series that first really put Portland on the professional racing map. When the series arrived in 1978, the IMSA cars were among the fastest and most exotic cars ever to race at PIR. In addition to the IMSA prototypes and IMSA light prototypes, the IMSA GTO, GTU, Escort Endurance, All-American Challenge, Firestone Firehawk, World Sports Car, and IMSA Supercar Series all raced at PIR over the years.

IMSA's Camel GT Series brought many well-known race car drivers to Portland, including Sam Posey, Hurley Haywood, Paul Newman, Bobby Rahal, Brian Redman, George Follmer, Janet Guthrie, and Lyn St. James, as well as local professional race car drivers Monte Shelton, Bill Craine, Herschel McGriff, and Parker Johnstone.

One of the most appealing things about IMSA GT racing was that the level of car preparation allowed was compatible with then-current club racing standards, so that local drivers could enter the events in their own cars. Local race car drivers such as Rich Sloma, Neil Shelton, Ted Mathey, Joe Chamberlain, Frank Poole, Charlie Hexom, Don Smethers, Ron Emmerson, Frank McKinnon, Dave Frezza, and others all entered IMSA races at PIR.

IMSA GT remained on the PIR schedule through 1994. After a five-year hiatus, IMSA sanctioning returned with the American Le Mans Series (ALMS), offering an entirely new formula and a new generation of cars from 1999 to 2001 and then again from 2004 to 2006.

The ALMS formula shifted IMSA's endurance racing tradition to a true Le Mans racing format, where many different performance classes raced at the same time in an endurance-style contest. In the years ALMS raced at PIR, the cars were divided into Prototype 1 and 2 classes and two classes of production-based cars, including Corvettes, Porsches, Ferraris, Aston Martins, and BMWs.

The purpose-built prototype racing cars were still the stars of the IMSA show in the ALMS era. But unlike the IMSA GTP machines that preceded them, ALMS prototypes are open-cockpit designs. The Le Mans Prototypes racing with ALMS included the revolutionary diesel-engined Audi R10 TDI machines that swept the series in 2006, including winning the Portland Grand Prix and the 24 Hours of Le Mans itself.

The No. 52 Lola T86 Corvette of Sarel van der Merwe and Doc Bundy leads the Ford Mustang Probe of Scott Pruett and Klaus Ludwig through turn No. 12 during the 1986 IMSA G.I. Joe's Portland Grand Prix. (Courtesy of OMMA.)

Drake Olsen (No. 98) in the Eagle HF89 Toyota leads Davy Jones (No. 60) in the Jaguar XJR-10 and Wayne Taylor in the Spice SE89P 003/Chevrolet during the 1990 IMSA G.I. Joe's Grand Prix. (Courtesy of Doug Berger.)

The No. 4 Spice Buick of Ken Knott and Jim Pace races the No. 83 Nissan NPT-90 of Geoff Brabham during the 1990 IMSA G.I. Joe's Grand Prix. (Courtesy of Doug Berger.)

Chip Robinson (No. 84) in the Nissan NPT-91 leads Juan Fangio II (No. 99) in the Eagle Mk III Toyota and the rest of the GTP field during the 1991 IMSA G.I. Joe's Grand Prix. (Courtesy of Doug Berger.)

The No. 10 Lotus Esprit X180R Turbo of Doc Bundy leads the field in the IMSA Supercar race during the 1992 G.I. Joe's Grand Prix. (Courtesy of Doug Berger.)

The Bud Light Jaguar of Davy Jones takes a pit stop during the 1992 G.I. Joe's Grand Prix. Jones went on to win the GTP race that day. (Courtesy of Doug Berger.)

The White Lightning Racing team of Robert Nagel, Wade Gaughran, Michael Petersen, and Dale White shared this Porsche 996 (No. 30) during the 2000 ALMS Rose City Grand Prix. (Courtesy of Jerry Boone.)

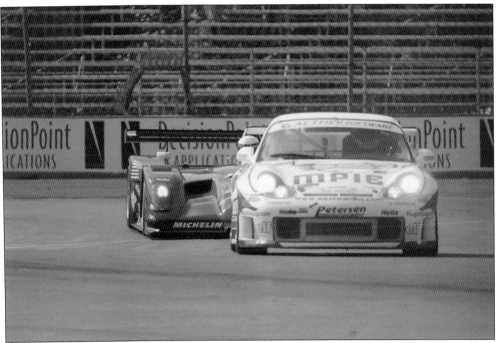

With cars of vastly different performance potential sharing the track for hours at a time, the American Le Mans Series tests drivers' endurance and their ability to manage traffic safely and effectively. (Courtesy of Jerry Boone.)

The No. 5 Porsche 996 of Dirk Müller and Lucas Lühr locks up a tire heading into the Festival Curves, with the No. 70 Porsche of David Murry and Johnny Mowlem close behind. (Courtesy of Jerry Boone.)

The No. 57 Reynard 01Q Le Mans Prototype of John Graham, Milka Duno, and Didier de Radigues is pictured during the 2001 Grand Prix of Portland. (Courtesy of Chris Greenwood.)

The Panoz LMP1 Roadster of Jan Magnussen and David Brabham took the overall win in the 2001 ALMS Grand Prix of Portland. (Courtesy of Chris Greenwood.)

The No. 38 Audi R8 of Andy Wallace and Johnny Herbert finished third in the 2001 ALMS Grand Prix of Portland, paving the way for the R10 to win everything in 2006. (Courtesy of Chris Greenwood.)

Today, IMSA cars of all generations are a popular feature at the Portland Historic Races. In this classic shot highlighting Mount Hood overlooking the track, Sam Moses (No. 44) drives his 1982 "Bandit" Oldsmobile. This is the same car he raced in the 1982 IMSA Kelly American Challenge Series. Moses's experience in the series inspired his iconic book *Fast Guys, Rich Guys, and Idiots: A Racing Odyssey on the Border of Obsession*. (Courtesy of Doug Berger.)

Seven

MOTORCYCLES

From the beginnings of PIR, motorcycle racing in its various forms has been an integral part of the facility's history. In the early 1960s, motorcyclists came together to race on the European sport bikes of the day. In 1972, local racers formed the Oregon Motorcycle Road Racing Association (OMRRA) and the organization continues to be the leading sanctioning body for motorcycle road-racing at PIR. Other current motorcycle-based organizations using PIR include Motocorsa, 2-Fast Motorcycles, and Pacific Super Sport Riders.

In addition to road-racing, PIR has been a site for motocross competition since the mid-1960s. The Wylder family has been involved since the beginning.

"Motocross actually started on the weekends about 1966. It did well and PIR was the only track around for miles. PIR started getting busy with weekend car events around 1970 so the PIR manager asked our father, Duane Wylder to take it over and run it for him on Thursday nights. He did, and it took off. It was the only nighttime motocross track in the nation. Our father at the time worked for Washougal and Fox Hollow MX and owned a motorcycle shop named Milwaukie Yamaha in the 1970s. He is now known as the 'Grandfather of Motocross' and has since retired. My brother Rick and I took it over in 2005 and brought new ideas to an old classic. It is now known as TNMX, or Thursday Night Motocross. It has been in the family for 47 years," says Ron Wylder.

The motocross track is located just northwest of the infield paddock, and the facility has undergone some changes over the years. The original control tower for the road-racing course was moved to the infield for motocross use when the PIR tower was built in the early 1970s.

"We have changed everything in and around the track in the last five-six years including a tower remodel we designed about 2010, a medic shack, more bleachers all around the track, tall wall and deck right behind the start line to reduce noise and add to the spectator experience," Wylder says.

The annual motocross course schedule includes 25 races from the first of April to the end of September. Each week's event serves from 800 to 2,000 people, for about 40,000 annual admissions.

Organized motorcycle racing began at PIR almost as soon as automobile racing. This photograph from 1963 shows the kind of small-displacement British and Italian motorcycles that were popular in that era. (Courtesy of OMMA.)

Sidecar racing has been a popular sport in several eras at PIR. Today, sidecar racing is sanctioned and organized by the Oregon Motorcycle Road Racing Association. (Courtesy of the PIR archive.)

Note the low-slung lay-down design of motorcycles used for sidecar racing. (Courtesy of the PIR archive.)

A race for Kawasaki two-stroke triple-cylinder motorcycles prepares to get underway in the 1970s. (Courtesy of OMMA.)

In the modern era, OMRRA races each month from April through September, providing a variety of classes for motorcycles of different sizes and levels of preparation. (Photograph by Jeff Zurschmeide.)

As motorcycle technology and design has improved, riders are safer and faster than ever. Motorcycle racers at PIR pioneered the use of Airfence soft barriers that are erected before every bike race. (Photograph by Jeff Zurschmeide.)

The original PIR tower is still in use at the motocross track every Thursday night. (Courtesy of the PIR archive.)

Motocross racing at PIR has been active since the mid-1960s. This rider (No. 266) is heading along the dike that separates the motocross area from the long slough that shapes and parallels the track's backstretch. (Courtesy of OMMA.)

PIR's motocross facility has been used by riders of all ages for decades. Riders as young as four years old enjoy the Thursday Night Motocross Series. (Courtesy of OMMA.)

The motocross facility also hosts an annual Race for a Cure, raising over $25,000 to date, to benefit breast cancer charities. (Photograph by Jeff Zurschmeide.)

Eight

PIR DRAG RACING

One of the less well-known facts about the history of PIR is that drag racing was a major driving force for track improvements in the late 1960s and early 1970s. PIR's first manager, Al Beachell, also managed the Woodburn drag strip.

Sanctioned drag racing at PIR began in the early 1960s, though clandestine racing also occurred earlier on the same streets. The fact that Cottonwood Street and Force Avenue both ran very nearly straight made them an attractive drag racing site.

However, both roads were limited to an eighth-mile course. In 1966, five major drag races were held at PIR, and the drag racing community asked the National Hot Rod Association (NHRA) to officially sanction the track.

In 1967, poor pavement conditions on Cottonwood Street pushed sanctioned drag racing onto Force Avenue. In 1969, drag racing returned to its original and current location when Cottonwood Street was repaved. This was the first part of the full track repaving, and it happened first because drag racing offered profitable and high-profile events. With 15 major drag races on the schedule, 1970 was the peak year for drag racing at PIR.

As part of the 1971 track restructuring, Cottonwood Street was straightened, and the shut down area was increased to allow for quarter-mile racing. At this time, the return road and staging lanes in the south paddock were paved. Construction began on April 27, and the first big race to occur on the new pavement was the Rose Festival Drags on June 5–6, 1971, followed later in the year by the NHRA Division 6 points meet.

Notable drag racing history at PIR includes Don Garlits's first five-second runs on July 7, 1973, at the Rainier Race of Champions event. Don Prudhomme clinched his first national championship in Funny Car at the Division 6 race at PIR in 1975. The fastest run in PIR history was a jet-powered car that traversed the quarter-mile in 4.804 seconds (ET) at 324.90 miles per hour.

PIR hosted a NHRA Division 6 points race from 1971 through 1980 and again in 1984 and 1985. In 1981, PIR switched from NHRA to American Hot Rod Association (AHRA) sanctioning. AHRA national events took place in 1982 and 1983 before the track returned to NHRA sanctioning in 1984.

Since 1985, drag racing at PIR has been limited to NHRA bracket racing on Wednesday nights, and since 2000, the quarter-mile Late Night Drags on Friday and Saturday nights.

Ironically, late-night drag racing was established to provide a safe alternative to illegal street racing—the same thing that used to take place in that very location.

Joe Clement of Washington campaigned this nitro-powered Chevrolet Monza funny car at PIR until 1978. (Courtesy of the PIR archive.)

In 2006, PIR obtained special permission for the Nitehawk jet-powered funny car to make several runs. The car is owned by Richard Smith and driven by Kyle Skidgel, both of Bend, Oregon. (Courtesy of David K. Brunn.)

Hot rods are among the most popular drag cars at PIR, especially during the Wednesday evening bracket drags that coincide with the Beaches Cruise-ins during the summer months. (Courtesy of Carol Brown.)

Whether they are running formal brackets or simply racing for fun on weekend nights, drag racing cars are some of the most creative and highly tuned racing vehicles one can find at the track. (Courtesy of Carol Brown.)

Although the Wednesday night bracket drags are a local event, many drivers who also compete at the divisional and national levels use these regular events to practice and tune-up for the major competitions. (Courtesy of Carol Brown.)

Father and son team Nick and Mike Nicholson line up in their Super Pro dragsters. State-of-the-art rail dragsters compete as well as stock and modified production-based cars. (Courtesy of Carol Brown.)

Cliff Waldron prepares to race his "No Taxi" Chevrolet. Noise limits and a 10:00 p.m. curfew on Wednesdays help keep PIR on good terms with its neighbors. On weekends, noise limits drop to street-legal levels of 90 decibels at 10:00 p.m., but racing continues until 1:00 a.m. (Photograph by Jeff Zurschmeide.)

In 2000, Portland experienced several fatal accidents due to illegal street racing, and on the suggestion of a Portland Police officer, PIR implemented late-night drag racing on Friday and Saturday nights from March through November. Anyone may come and drag race any car for a nominal fee. Portland has had no deaths due to street racing since the Late Night Drags were instituted. (Courtesy of Carol Brown.)

Electric-powered drag racing is a popular event each summer. In this photograph, the KillaCycle electric drag racing motorcycle shows off its power in the burnout box. KillaCycle is driven by Scotty Pollacheck and owned by Bill Dubé. (Courtesy of Carol Brown.)

John Wayland's White Zombie electric drag racing car is one of the best-known electric drag racing machines in the United States. Wayland has received substantial sponsorship and performed groundbreaking research into electric racing. (Photograph by Carol Brown.)

Past Winners

The following race winners are just a tiny number of the thousands of men and women who have competed in races at PIR. Winners get the glory and the bouquet of roses, but race fans should always remember that it is the rest of the field that makes the victory possible.

NASCAR

NASCAR K&N Pro Series West	August 24, 1986	Hershel McGriff
NASCAR Northwest Series	June 24, 1995	Mark Martin
NASCAR Northwest Series	June 22, 1996	Lance Hooper
NASCAR Northwest Series	June 21, 1997	Tom Hubert
NASCAR Northwest Series	June 20, 1998	Rudy Revak
NASCAR Northwest Series	April 22, 2000	John Zaretzke
NASCAR Northwest Series	June 23, 2001	Gary Lewis
NASCAR Craftsman (now Camping World) Truck Series	June 18, 1999	Greg Biffle
NASCAR Craftsman (now Camping World) Truck Series	April 22, 2000	Andy Houston
NASCAR K&N Pro Series West	July 19, 2009	Jim Inglebright
NASCAR K&N Pro Series West	July 18, 2010	Patrick Long
NASCAR K&N Pro Series West	July 24, 2011	Luis Martinez Jr.
NASCAR K&N Pro Series West	August 26, 2012	Greg Pursley

CART/Champ Car World Series

CART	June 17, 1984	Al Unser Jr.
CART	June 16, 1985	Mario Andretti
CART	June 15, 1986	Mario Andretti
CART	June 14, 1987	Bobby Rahal
CART	June 19, 1988	Danny Sullivan
CART	June 25, 1989	Emerson Fittipaldi
CART	June 24, 1990	Michael Andretti
CART	June 23, 1991	Michael Andretti
CART	June 21, 1992	Michael Andretti
CART	June 27, 1993	Emerson Fittipaldi
CART	June 26, 1994	Al Unser Jr.
CART	June 25, 1995	Al Unser Jr.
CART	June 23, 1996	Alex Zanardi
CART	June 22, 1997	Mark Blundell
CART	June 21, 1998	Alex Zanardi
CART	June 20, 1999	Gil de Ferran
CART	June 25, 2000	Gil de Ferran
CART	July 24, 2001	Max Papis
CART	June 16, 2002	Cristiano da Matta
CART	June 22, 2003	Adrian Fernandez
CCWS	June 20, 2004	Sébastien Bourdais
CCWS	June 19, 2005	Cristiano da Matta
CCWS	June 18, 2006	AJ Allmendinger
CCWS	June 10, 2007	Sébastien Bourdais

SCCA Trans-Am

Trans-Am—September 17, 1972—John Morton

Trans-Am—June 15, 1975—John Greenwood

Trans-Am—June 13, 1976—Monte Shelton (Cat II)

Trans-Am—June 13, 1976—Joe Chamberlain (Cat I)

Trans-Am—June 12, 1977—George Follmer (Cat II)

Trans-Am—June 12, 1977—John Bauer (Cat I)

Trans-Am—June 11, 1978—Tuck Thomas (Cat II)

Trans-Am—June 11, 1978—Bob Matkovich (Cat I)

Trans-Am—June 10, 1979—John Paul (Cat II)

Trans-Am—June 10, 1979—Gene Bothello (Cat I)

Trans-Am—June 15, 1980—Mark Pielsticker

Trans-Am—June 14, 1981—Bob Tullius

Trans-Am—June 13, 1982—Doc Bundy

Trans-Am—June 12, 1983—Willy T. Ribbs

Trans-Am—June 14, 1984—Greg Pickett

Trans-Am—June 15, 1985—Wally Dallenbach Jr.

Trans-Am—June 14, 1986—Wally Dallenbach Jr.

Trans-Am—June 7, 1987—Pete Halsmer

Trans-Am—June 23, 1990—Darin Brassfield

Trans-Am—June 22, 1991—Irv Hoerr

Trans-Am—June 20, 1992—Paul Gentilozzi

Trans-Am—June 26, 1993—Ron Fellows

Trans-Am—June 25, 1994—Ron Fellows

Trans-Am—June 24, 1995—Ron Fellows

Trans-Am—June 23, 2001—Tommy Archer

Trans-Am—June 19, 2004—Paul Gentilozzi

Trans-Am—June 18, 2005—Klaus Graf

Trans-Am—June 14, 2009—Tomy Drissi

IMSA CAMEL GT and ALMS

IMSA GT	August 6 ,1978	Peter Gregg
IMSA GT	August 5, 1979	Peter Gregg
IMSA GT	August 3, 1980	John Fitzpatrick
IMSA GT	August 2, 1981	Brian Redman
IMSA GT	August 1, 1982	John Paul Jr.
IMSA GT	July 31, 1983	Al Holbert
IMSA GT	July 28, 1984	Randy Lanier/Bill Whittington
IMSA GT	July 28, 1985	Al Holbert
IMSA GT	July 27, 1986	Al Holbert
IMSA GT	July 26, 1987	Chip Robinson
IMSA GT	July 31, 1988	Geoff Brabham
IMSA GT	July 30, 1989	Jan Lammers/Price Cobb
IMSA GT	July 29 1990	Davy Jones
IMSA GT	July 28, 1991	Juan Fangio II
IMSA GT	July 25, 1992	P.J. Jones
IMSA GT	August 1, 1993	Juan Fangio II
IMSA GT˙	August 7, 1994	Steve Millen
ALMS	August 1, 1999	David Brabham/Eric Bernard
ALMS	September 10, 2000	Rinaldo Capello/Allan McNish
ALMS	July 25, 2004	JJ Lehto/Marco Werner
ALMS	July 30, 2005	Frank Biela/Emanuele Pirro
ALMS	July 22, 2006	Rinaldo Capello/Allan McNish

Rose Cup Winners

Year	Winner	Year	Winner
1961	Jerry Grant	1988	Monte Shelton
1962	Jerry Grant	1989	Steve Petty
1963	Bill Stephens	1990	Steve Petty
1964	Pierre Phillips	1991	Stuart Hayner
1965	John Hall	1992	Jeff Davis
1966	David Phelan	1993	Brian Richards
1967	Bill Amick	1994	Brian Richards
1968	Stan Burnett	1995	Steve Hodge
1969	Jon Milledge	1996	Steve Hodge
1970	Milt Minter	1997	Steve Hodge
1971	Herb Caplan	1998	Steve Hodge
1972	Monte Shelton	1999	Mike Rockett
1973	Bill Cuddy	2000	Frank Emmett
1974	Monte Shelton	2001	Frank Emmett
1975	John Greenwood	2002	Frank Emmett
1976	Monte Shelton	2003	Frank Emmett
1977	George Follmer	2004	Steve Hodge
1978	Tuck Thomas	2005	Monte Shelton
1979	John Paul	2006	Steve Hodge
1980	Mark Pielsticker	2007	Todd Harris
1981	Bob Tullius	2008	Neil Shelton
1982	Doc Bundy	2009	Tomy Drissi
1983	Willy T. Ribbs	2010	Matt Crandall
1984	Monte Shelton	2011	Brian Richards
1985	Bob Schrader	2012	Matt Crandall
1986	Monte Shelton	2013	Matt Crandall
1987	Pete Halsmer		

Discover Thousands of Local History Books Featuring Millions of Vintage Images

Arcadia Publishing, the leading local history publisher in the United States, is committed to making history accessible and meaningful through publishing books that celebrate and preserve the heritage of America's people and places.

Find more books like this at
www.arcadiapublishing.com

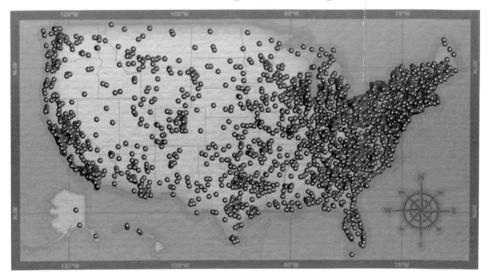

Search for your hometown history, your old stomping grounds, and even your favorite sports team.